THE ELEMENTS OF STYLE

WILLIAM STRUNK

SANAGE
PUBLISHING HOUSE

Paperback: 978-811900780-6

Printed by: Manipal Technologies Limited, Manipal

Sanage Publishing House LLP
Mumbai, India

sanagepublishing@gmail.com

William Strunk Jr. (July 1, 1869 – September 26, 1946) was an American professor of English at Cornell University and author of The Elements of Style (1918). After revision and enlargement by his former student E. B. White, it became a highly influential guide to English usage during the late 20th century, commonly called Strunk & White.

CONTENTS

I. INTRODUCTORY 5

II. ELEMENTARY RULES OF USAGE 7

III. ELEMENTARY PRINCIPLES OF COMPOSITION 16

IV. A FEW MATTERS OF FORM 38

V. WORDS AND EXPRESSIONS COMMONLY MISUSED 42

VI. SPELLING 56

I. INTRODUCTORY

This book aims to give in brief space the principal requirements of plain English style. It aims to lighten the task of instructor and student by concentrating attention (in Chapters II and III) on a few essentials, the rules of usage and principles of composition most commonly violated. In accordance with this plan, it lays down three rules for the use of the comma, instead of a score or more, and one for the use of the semicolon, in the belief that these four rules provide for all the internal punctuation that is required by nineteen sentences out of twenty. Similarly, it gives in Chapter III only those principles of the paragraph and the sentence which are of the widest application. The book thus covers only a small portion of the field of English style. The experience of its writer has been that once past the essentials, students profit most by individual instruction based on the problems of their own work, and that each instructor has his own body of theory, which he may prefer to that offered by any textbook.

The numbers of the sections may be used as references in correcting manuscript.

The writer's colleagues in the Department of English in Cornell University have greatly helped him in the preparation of his manuscript. Mr. George McLane Wood has kindly consented to the inclusion under Rule 10 of some material from his Suggestions to Authors.

The following books are recommended for reference or further study: in connection with Chapters II and IV, F. Howard Collins, *Author and Printer* (Henry Frowde); Chicago University Press, *Manual of Style*; T. L. De Vinne, *Correct Composition* (The Century Company); Horace Hart, *Rules for Compositors* and Printers (Oxford University Press); George McLane Wood, *Extracts from the Style-Book of the Government Printing Office* (United States Geological Survey); in connection with Chapters III and V, *The King's English* (Oxford University Press); Sir Arthur Quiller-Couch, *The Art of Writing* (Putnam), especially the chapter, Interlude on Jargon; George McLane Wood, *Suggestions to Authors* (United States Geological Survey); John Lesslie Hall, *English Usage* (Scott, Foresman and Co.); James P. Kelley, *Workmanship in Words* (Little, Brown and Co.). In these will be found full discussions of many points here briefly treated and an abundant store of illustrations to supplement those given in this book.

It is an old observation that the best writers sometimes disregard the rules of rhetoric. When they do so, however, the reader will usually find in the sentence some compensating merit, attained at the cost of the violation. Unless he is certain of doing as well, he will probably do best to follow the rules. After he has learned, by their guidance, to write plain English adequate for everyday uses, let him look, for the secrets of style, to the study of the Master of Literature.

II. ELEMENTARY RULES OF USAGE

1. Form the possessive singular of nouns by adding 's.

Follow this rule whatever the final consonant. Thus write,

Charles's friend

Burns's poems

the witch's malice

This is the usage of the United States Government Printing Office and of the Oxford University Press.

Exceptions are the possessive of ancient proper names in -es and -*is*, the possessive *Jesus*', and such forms as *for conscience*' *sake*, *for righteousness*' *sake*. But such forms as *Achilles*' *heel*, *Moses*' *laws*, *Isis*' temple are commonly replaced by,

the heel of Achilles

the laws of Moses

the temple of Isis

The pronominal possessives *hers*, *its*, *theirs*, *yours*, and *oneself* have no apostrophe.

2. In a series of three or more terms with a single conjunction, use a comma after each term except the last.

Thus write,

red, white, and blue

gold, silver, or copper

He opened the letter, read it, and made a note of its contents.

This is also the usage of the Government Printing Office and of the Oxford University Press.

In the names of business firms, the last comma is omitted, as,

Brown, Shipley & Co.

3. Enclose parenthetic expressions between commas.

The best way to see a country, unless you are pressed for time, is to travel on foot.

This rule is difficult to apply; it is frequently hard to decide whether a single word, such as *however,* or a brief phrase, is or is not parenthetic. If the interruption to the flow of the sentence is but slight, the writer may safely omit the commas. But whether the interruption be slight or considerable, he must never insert one comma and omit the other. Such punctuation as

Marjorie's husband, Colonel Nelson paid us a visit yesterday,

or

My brother you will be pleased to hear, is now in perfect health is indefensible.

If a parenthetic expression is preceded by a conjunction, place the first comma before the conjunction, not after it.

He saw us coming and unaware that we had learned of his treachery, greeted us with a smile.

Always to be regarded as parenthetic and to be enclosed between commas (or, at the end of the sentence, between comma and period) are the following:

(1) the year, when forming part of a date, and the day of the month, when following the day of the week:

February to July 1916.

April 6, 1917.

Monday, November 11, 1918.

(2) the abbreviations *etc.* and *jr.*

(3) non-restrictive relative clauses, that is, those which do not serve to identify or define the antecedent noun, and similar clauses introduced by conjunctions indicating time or place.

The audience, which had at first been indifferent, became more and more interested.

In this sentence the clause introduced by *which* does not serve to tell which of several possible audiences is meant; what audience is in question is supposed to be already known. The clause adds, parenthetically, a statement supplementing that in the main clause. The sentence is virtually a combination of two statements which might have been made independently:

The audience had at first been indifferent. It became more and more interested.

Compare the restrictive relative clause, not set off by commas, in the sentence,

The candidate who best meets these requirements will obtain the place.

Here the clause introduced by *who* does serve to tell which of several possible candidates is meant; the sentence cannot be split up into two independent statements.

The difference in punctuation in the two sentences following is based on the same principle:

Nether Stowey, where Coleridge wrote *The Rime of the Ancient Mariner,* is a few miles from Bridgewater.

The day will come when you will admit your mistake.

Nether Stowey is completely identified by its name; the statement about Coleridge is therefore supplementary and parenthetic. The day spoken of is identified only by the dependent clause, which is therefore restrictive.

Similar in principle to the enclosing of parenthetic expressions between commas is the setting off by commas of phrases or dependent clauses preceding or following the main clause of a sentence.

Partly by hard fighting, partly by diplomatic skill, they enlarged their dominions to the east and rose to royal rank with the possession of Sicily, exchanged afterwards for Sardinia.

Other illustrations may be found in sentences quoted under Rules 4, 5, 6, 7, 16, and 18.

The writer should be careful not to set off independent clauses by commas: see under Rule 5.

4. Place a comma before a conjunction introducing a co-ordinate clause.

The early records of the city have disappeared, and the story of its first years can no longer be reconstructed.

The situation is perilous but there is still one chance of escape.

Sentences of this type, isolated from their context, may seem to be in need of rewriting. As they make complete sense when the comma is reached, the second clause has the appearance of an afterthought. Further, *and* is the least specific of connectives. Used between independent clauses, it indicates only that a relation exists between them without defining that relation. In the example above, the relation is that of cause and result. The two sentences might be rewritten:

As the early records of the city have disappeared, the story of its first years can no longer be reconstructed.

Although the situation is perilous, there is still one chance of escape.

Or the subordinate clauses might be replaced by phrases:

Owing to the disappearance of the early records of the city, the story of its first years can no longer be reconstructed.

In this perilous situation, there is still one chance of escape.

But a writer may err by making his sentences too uniformly compact and periodic, and an occasional loose sentence prevents the style from becoming too formal and gives the reader a certain relief. Consequently, loose sentences of the type first quoted are common in easy, unstudied writing. But a writer should be careful not to construct too many of his sentences after this pattern (see Rule 14).

Two-part sentences of which the second member is introduced by as (in the sense of *because*), *for, or, nor,* and *while* (in the sense of *and at the same time*) likewise require a comma before the conjunction.

If the second member is introduced by an adverb, a semicolon, not a comma, is required (see Rule 5). The connectives so and yet may be used either as adverbs or as conjunctions, accordingly as the second clause is felt to be co-ordinate or subordinate; consequently either mark of punctuation may be justified. But these uses of so (equivalent to *accordingly* or to *so that*) are somewhat colloquial and should, as a rule, be avoided in writing. A simple correction, usually serviceable, is to omit the word so and begin the first clause with *as* or *since:*

I had never been in the place before; so; I had difficulty in finding my way about.

As I had never been in the place before, I had difficulty in finding my way about.

If a dependent clause, or an introductory phrase requiring to be set off by a comma, precedes the second independent clause, no comma is needed after the conjunction.

The situation is perilous, but if we are prepared to act promptly, there is still one chance of escape.

When the subject is the same for both clauses and is expressed only once, a comma is required if the connective is *but*. If the connective is and, the comma should be omitted if the relation between the two statements is close or immediate.

I have heard his arguments but am still unconvinced.

He has had several years' experience and is thoroughly competent.

5. Do not join independent clauses by a comma.

If two or more clauses, grammatically complete and not joined by a conjunction, are to form a single compound sentence, the proper mark of punctuation is a semicolon.

Stevenson's romances are entertaining; they are full of exciting adventures.

It is nearly half past five; we cannot reach town before dark.

It is of course equally correct to write the above as two sentences each, replacing the semicolons by periods.

Stevenson's romances are entertaining. They are full of exciting adventures.

It is nearly half past five. We cannot reach town before dark.

If a conjunction is inserted the proper mark is a comma (Rule 4).

Stevenson's romances are entertaining, for they are full of exciting adventures.

It is nearly half past five, and we cannot reach town before dark.

A comparison of the three forms given above will clearly show the advantage of the first. It is, at least in the examples given, better than the second form, because it suggests the close relationship between the two statements in a way that the second does not attempt, and better than the third, because briefer and therefore more forcible. Indeed, it may be said that this simple method of indicating relationship between statements is one of the most useful devices of composition. The relationship, as above, is commonly one of cause or of consequence.

Note that if the second clause is preceded by an adverb, such as *accordingly, besides, then, therefore,* or *thus* and not by a conjunction, the semicolon is still required.

Two exceptions to the rule may be admitted. If the clauses are very short, and are alike in form, a comma is usually permissible:

Man proposes, God disposes.

The gate swung apart, the bridge fell, the portcullis was drawn up.

Note that in these examples the relation is not one of cause or consequence. Also, in the colloquial form of expression,

I hardly knew him, he was so changed,

a comma, not a semicolon, is required. But this form of expression is inappropriate in writing, except in the dialogue of a story or play, or perhaps in a familiar letter.

6. Do not break sentences in two.

In other words, do not use periods for commas.

I met them on a Cunard liner several years ago. Coming home from

Liverpool to New York.

He was an interesting talker. A man who had traveled all over the world and lived in half a dozen countries.

In both these examples, the first period should be replaced by a comma, and the following word begun with a small letter.

It is permissible to make an emphatic word or expression serve the purpose of a sentence and to punctuate it accordingly:

Again and Again, he called out. No reply.

The writer must, however, be certain that the emphasis is warranted, and that he will not be suspected of a mere blunder in syntax or in punctuation.

Rules 3, 4, 5, and 6 cover the most important principles in the punctuation of ordinary sentences; they should be so thoroughly mastered that their application becomes second nature.

7. A participial phrase at the beginning of a sentence must refer to the grammatical subject

Walking slowly down the road, he saw a woman accompanied by two children.

The word walking refers to the subject of the sentence, not to the woman. If the writer wishes to make it refer to the woman, he must recast the sentence:

He saw a woman accompanied by two children, walking slowly down the road.

Participial phrases preceded by a conjunction or by a preposition, nouns in apposition, adjectives, and adjective phrases come under the same rule if they begin the sentence.

On arriving in Chicago, his friends met him at the station.

When he arrived (or, On his arrival) in Chicago, his friends met

him at the station.

A soldier of proved valor, they entrusted him with the defence of the city.

A soldier of proved valor, he was entrusted with the defence of the city.

Young and inexperienced, the task seemed easy to me.

Young and inexperienced, I thought the task easy.

Without a friend to counsel him, the temptation proved irresistible.

Without a friend to counsel him, he found the temptation irresistible.

Sentences violating this rule are often ludicrous.

Being in a dilapidated condition, I was able to buy the house very cheap.

Wondering irresolutely what to do next, the clock struck twelve.

III. ELEMENTARY PRINCIPLES OF COMPOSITION

8. Make the paragraph the unit of composition: one paragraph to each topic.

If the subject on which you are writing is of slight extent, or if you intend to treat it very briefly, there may be no need of subdividing it into topics. Thus, a brief description, a brief summary of a literary work, a brief account of a single incident, a narrative merely outlining an action, the setting forth of a single idea, any one of these is best written in a single paragraph. After the paragraph has been written, examine it to see whether subdivision will not improve it.

Ordinarily, however, a subject requires subdivision into topics, each of which should be made the subject of a paragraph. The object of treating each topic in a paragraph by itself is, of course, to aid the reader. The beginning of each paragraph is a signal to him that a new step in the development of the subject has been reached.

The extent of subdivision will vary with the length of the composition. For example, a short notice of a book or poem might consist of a single paragraph. One slightly longer might consist of two paragraphs:

- A. Account of the work.

- B. Critical discussion.

A report on a poem, written for a class in literature, might consist of seven paragraphs:

- A. Facts of composition and publication.
- B. Kind of poem; metrical form.
- C. Subject.
- D. Treatment of subject.
- E. For what chiefly remarkable.
- F. Wherein characteristic of the writer.
- G. Relationship to other works.

The contents of paragraphs C and D would vary with the poem. Usually, paragraph C would indicate the actual or imagined circumstances of the poem (the situation), if these call for explanation, and would then state the subject and outline its development. If the poem is a narrative in the third person throughout, paragraph C need contain no more than a concise summary of the action. Paragraph D would indicate the leading ideas and show how they are made prominent or would indicate what points in the narrative are chiefly emphasized.

A novel might be discussed under the heads:

- A. Setting.
- B. Plot.
- C. Characters.
- D. Purpose.

An historical event might be discussed under the heads:

- A. What led up to the event.
- B. Account of the event.

- C. What the event led up to.

In treating either of these last two subjects, the writer would probably find it necessary to subdivide one or more of the topics here given.

As a rule, single sentences should not be written or printed as paragraphs. An exception may be made of sentences of transition, indicating the relation between the parts of an exposition or argument. Frequent exceptions are also necessary in textbooks, guidebooks, and other works in which many topics are treated briefly.

In dialogue, each speech, even if only a single word, is a paragraph by itself; that is, a new paragraph begins with each change of speaker. The application of this rule, when dialogue and narrative are combined, is best learned from examples in well-printed works of fiction.

9. As a rule, begin each paragraph with a topic sentence, end it in conformity with the beginning.

Again, the object is to aid the reader. The practice here recommended enables him to discover the purpose of each paragraph as he begins to read it, and to retain this purpose in mind as he ends it. For this reason, the most generally useful kind of paragraph, particularly in exposition and argument, is that in which.

(a) the topic sentence comes at or near the beginning

(b) the succeeding sentences explain or establish or develop the statement made in the topic sentence and

(c) the final sentence either emphasizes the thought of the topic sentence or states some important consequence.

Ending with a digression, or with an unimportant detail, is particularly to be avoided.

If the paragraph forms part of a larger composition, its relation to what precedes, or its function as a part of the whole, may need to be expressed. This can sometimes be done by a mere word or phrase (*again; therefore, for the same reason*) in the topic sentence. Sometimes, however, it is expedient to precede the topic sentence by one or more sentences of introduction or transition. If more than one such sentence is required, it is generally better to set apart the transitional sentences as a separate paragraph.

According to the writer's purpose, he may, as indicated above, relate the body of the paragraph to the topic sentence in one or more of several different ways. He may make the meaning of the topic sentence clearer by restating it in other forms, by defining its terms, by denying the contrary, by giving illustrations or specific instances; he may establish it by proofs, or he may develop it by showing its implications and consequences. In a long paragraph, he may carry out several of these processes.

1 Now, to be properly enjoyed, a walking tour should be gone upon alone.

2 If you go in a company, or even in pairs, it is no longer a walking tour in anything but name; it is something else and more in the nature of a picnic.

3 A walking tour should be gone upon alone, because freedom is of the essence; because you should be able to stop and go on, and follow this way or that, as the freak takes you; and because you must have your own pace, and neither trot alongside a champion walker, nor mince in time with a girl.

4 And you must be open to all impressions and let your thoughts take colour from what you see.

5 You should be as a pipe for any wind to play upon.

6 "I cannot see the wit," says Hazlitt, "of walking and talking at the same time.

7 When I am in the country, I wish to vegetate like the country," which is the gist of all that can be said upon the matter.

8 There should be no cackle of voices at your elbow, to jar on the meditative silence of the morning.

9 And so long as a man is reasoning he cannot surrender himself to that fine intoxication that comes of much motion in the open air, that begins in a sort of dazzle and sluggishness of the brain, and ends in a peace that passes comprehension.....Stevenson, *Walking Tours.*

1 Topic sentence.

2 The meaning made clearer by denial of the contrary.

3 The topic sentence repeated, in abridged form, and supported by three reasons; the meaning of the third ("you must have your own pace") made clearer by denying the contrary.

4 A fourth reason, stated in two forms.

5 The same reason, stated in still another form.

6–7 The same reason as stated by Hazlitt.

8 Repetition, in paraphrase, of the quotation from Hazlitt.

9 Final statement of the fourth reason, in language amplified and heightened to form a strong conclusion.

1 It was chiefly in the eighteenth century that a very different conception of history grew up.

2 Historians then came to believe that their task was not so much to paint a picture as to solve a problem; to explain or illustrate the successive phases of national growth, prosperity, and adversity.

3 The history of morals, of industry, of intellect, and of art; the changes that take place in manners or beliefs; the dominant ideas that prevailed in successive periods; the rise, fall, and modification of political constitutions; in a word, all the conditions of national well-being became the subject of their works.

4 They sought rather to write a history of peoples than a history of

kings.

5 They looked especially in history for the chain of causes and effects.

6 They undertook to study in the past the physiology of nations, and hoped by applying the experimental method on a large scale to deduce some lessons of real value about the conditions on which the welfare of society mainly depend.—Lecky, *The Political Value of History.*

1 Topic sentence.

2 The meaning of the topic sentence made clearer; the new conception of history defined.

3 The definition expanded.

4 The definition explained by contrast.

5 The definition supplemented: another element in the new conception of history.

6 Conclusion: an important consequence of the new conception of history.

In narration and description, the paragraph sometimes begins with a concise, comprehensive statement serving to hold together the details that follow.

The breeze served us admirably.

The campaign opened with a series of reverses.

The next ten or twelve pages were filled with a curious set of entries.

But this device, if too often used, would become a mannerism. More commonly the opening sentence simply indicates by its subject with what the paragraph is to be principally concerned.

At length I thought I might return towards the stockade.

He picked up the heavy lamp from the table and began to explore.

Another flight of steps, and they emerged on the roof.

The brief paragraphs of animated narrative, however, are often without even this semblance of a topic sentence. The break between them serves the purpose of a rhetorical pause, throwing into prominence some detail of the action.

10. Use the active voice.

The active voice is usually more direct and vigorous than the passive:

I shall always remember my first visit to Boston.

This is much better than

My first visit to Boston will always be remembered by me.

The latter sentence is less direct, less bold, and less concise. If the writer tries to make it more concise by omitting "by me,"

My first visit to Boston will always be remembered,

it becomes indefinite: is it the writer, or some person undisclosed, or the world at large, that will always remember this visit?

This rule does not, of course, mean that the writer should entirely discard the passive voice, which is frequently convenient and sometimes necessary.

The dramatists of the Restoration are little esteemed today.

Modern readers have little esteem for the dramatists of the Restoration.

The first would be the right form in a paragraph on the dramatists of the Restoration; the second, in a paragraph on the tastes of modern readers. The need of making a particular word the subject of the sentence will often, as in these examples, determine which voice is to be used.

As a rule, avoid making one passive depend directly upon another.

Gold was not allowed to be exported.

It was forbidden to export gold (The export of gold was prohibited).

He has been proved to have been seen entering the building.

It has been proved that he was seen to enter the building.

In both the examples above, before correction, the word properly related to the second passive is made the subject of the first.

A common fault is to use as the subject of a passive construction a noun which expresses the entire action, leaving to the verb no function beyond that of completing the sentence.

A survey of this region was made in 1900.

This region was surveyed in 1900.

Mobilization of the army was rapidly effected.

The army was rapidly mobilized.

Confirmation of these reports cannot be obtained.

These reports cannot be confirmed.

Compare the sentence, "The export of gold was prohibited," in which the predicate "was prohibited" expresses something not implied in "export."

The habitual use of the active voice makes for forcible writing. This is true not only in narrative principally concerned with action, but in writing of any kind. Many a tame sentence of description or exposition can be made lively and emphatic by substituting a verb in the active voice for some such perfunctory expression as *there is* or *could be heard.*

There were a great number of dead leaves lying on the ground.

Dead leaves covered the ground.

The sound of a guitar somewhere in the house could be heard.

Somewhere in the house a guitar hummed sleepily.

The reason that he left college was that his health became impaired.

Failing health compelled him to leave college.

It was not long before he was very sorry that he had said what he had.

He soon repented his words.

11. Put statements in positive form.

Make definite assertions. Avoid tame, colorless, hesitating, non-committal language. Use the word not as a means of denial or in antithesis, never as a means of evasion.

He was not very often on time.

He usually came late.

He did not think that studying Latin was much use.

He thought the study of Latin useless.

***The Taming of the Shrew* is rather weak in spots. Shakespeare does not portray Katharine as a very admirable character, nor does Bianca remain long in memory as an important character in Shakespeare's works.**

The women in *The Taming of the Shrew* are unattractive. Katharine is disagreeable, Bianca insignificant.

The last example, before correction, is indefinite as well as negative. The corrected version, consequently, is simply a guess at the writer's intention.

All three examples show the weakness inherent in the word *not*.

Consciously or unconsciously, the reader is dissatisfied with being told only what is not; he wishes to be told what is. Hence, as a rule, it is better to express even a negative in positive form.

not honest	dishonest
not important	trifling
did not remember	forgot
did not pay any attention to	ignored
did not have much confidence in	distrusted

The antithesis of negative and positive is strong:

Not charity, but simple justice.

Not that I loved Caesar less, but Rome the more.

Negative words other than *not* are usually strong:

The sun never sets upon the British flag.

12. Use definite, specific, concrete language.

Prefer the specific to the general, the definite to the vague, the concrete to the abstract.

A period of unfavorable weather set in.

It rained every day for a week.

He showed satisfaction as he took possession of his well-earned reward.

He grinned as he pocketed the coin.

There is a general agreement among those who have enjoyed the experience that surf-riding is productive of great exhilaration.

All who have tried surf-riding agree that it is most

exhilarating.

If those who have studied the art of writing are in accord on any one point, it is on this, that the surest method of arousing and holding the attention of the reader is by being specific, definite, and concrete. Critics have pointed out how much of the effectiveness of the greatest writers, Homer, Dante, Shakespeare, results from their constant definiteness and concreteness. Browning, to cite a more modern author, offers many striking examples. Take, for instance, the lines from *My Last Duchess,*

Sir, 'twas all one! My favour at her breast,

The dropping of the daylight in the west,

The bough of cherries some officious fool

Broke in the orchard for her, the white mule,

She rode with round the terrace all and each,

Would draw from her alike the approving speech,

Or blush, at least,

and those which end the poem,

Notice Neptune, though,

Taming a seahorse, thought a rarity,

Which Claus of Innsbruck cast in bronze for me.

These words call up pictures. Recall how in *The Bishop Orders his Tomb in St. Praxed's Church* "the Renaissance spirit its worldliness, inconsistency, pride, hypocrisy, ignorance of itself, love of art, of luxury, of good Latin," to quote Ruskin's comment on the poem, is made manifest in specific details and in concrete terms.

Prose, in particular narrative and descriptive prose, is made vivid by the same means. If the experiences of Jim Hawkins and of David Balfour, of Kim, of Nostromo, have seemed for the moment real to countless readers, if in reading Carlyle we have almost the sense of being physically present at the taking of the Bastille, it is because of the definiteness of the details and the concreteness of the terms used. It is not that every detail is given; that would be impossible, as well as to no purpose but that all the significant details are given, and not vaguely but with such definiteness that the reader, in imagination, can project himself into the scene.

In exposition and in argument, the writer must likewise never lose his hold upon the concrete, and even when he is dealing with general principles, he must give particular instances of their application.

"This superiority of specific expressions is clearly due to the effort required to translate words into thoughts. As we do not think in generals, but in particulars as whenever any class of things is referred to, we represent it to ourselves by calling to mind individual members of it, it follows that when an abstract word is used, the hearer or reader has to choose, from his stock of images, one or more by which he may figure to himself the genus mentioned. In doing this, some delay must arise, some force be expended; and if by employing a specific term an appropriate image can be at once suggested, an economy is achieved, and a more vivid impression produced."

Herbert Spencer, from whose *Philosophy of Style* the preceding paragraph is quoted, illustrates the principle by the sentences:

In proportion as the manners, customs, and amusements of a nation are cruel and barbarous, the regulations of their penal code will be severe.

In proportion as men delight in battles, bullfights, and combats of gladiators, will they punish by hanging, burning, and the rack.

13. Omit needless words.

Vigorous writing is concise. A sentence should contain no unnecessary words, a paragraph no unnecessary sentences, for the same reason that a drawing should have no unnecessary lines and a machine no unnecessary parts. This requires not that the writer make all his sentences short, or that he avoid all detail and treat his subjects only in outline, but that he make every word tell.

Many expressions in common use violate this principle:

the question as to whether	**whether (the question whether)**
there is no doubt but that	**no doubt (doubtless)**
used for fuel purposes	**used for fuel**
he is a man who	**he**
in a hasty manner	**hastily**
this is a subject which	**this subject**
His story is a strange one.	**His story is strange.**

In especially the expression the fact that should be revised out of every sentence in which it occurs.

owing to the fact that	**since (because)**
in spite of the fact that	**though (although)**
call your attention to the fact that	**remind you (notify you)**
I was unaware of the fact that	**I was unaware that (did not know)**
the fact that he had not succeeded	**his failure**
the fact that I had arrived	**my arrival**

See also under *case, character, nature, system* in Chapter V.

Who is, which was, and the like are often superfluous.

His brother, who is a member of the same firm

His brother, a member of the same firm

Trafalgar, which was Nelson's last battle

Trafalgar, Nelson's last battle

As positive statement is more concise than negative, and the active voice more concise than the passive, many of the examples given under Rules 11 and 12 illustrate this rule as well.

A common violation of conciseness is the presentation of a single complex idea, step by step, in a series of sentences or independent clauses which might to advantage be combined into one.

Macbeth was very ambitious. This led him to wish to become king of Scotland. The witches told him that this wish of his would come true. The king of Scotland at this time was Duncan. Encouraged by his wife, Macbeth murdered Duncan. He was thus enabled to succeed Duncan as king. (51 words.)

Encouraged by his wife, Macbeth achieved his ambition and realized the prediction of the witches by murdering Duncan and becoming king of Scotland in his place. (26 words.)

There were several less important courses, but these were the most important, and although they did not come every day, they came often enough to keep you in such a state of mind that you never knew what your next move would be. (43 words.)

These, the most important courses of all, came, if not daily, at least often enough to keep one under constant strain. (21 words.)

14. Avoid a succession of loose sentences:

This rule refers especially to loose sentences of a particular type, those consisting of two co-ordinate clauses, the second introduced by a conjunction or relative. Although single sentences of this type may be unexceptionable (see under Rule 4), a series soon becomes monotonous and tedious.

An unskillful writer will sometimes construct a whole paragraph of sentences of this kind, using as connectives and, but, so and less frequently, *who, which, when, where,* and *while*, these last in non-restrictive senses (see under Rule 3).

The third concert of the subscription series was given last evening, and a large audience was in attendance. Mr. Edward Appleton was the soloist, and the Boston Symphony Orchestra furnished the instrumental music. The former showed himself to be an artist of the first rank, while the latter proved itself fully deserving of its high reputation. The interest aroused by the series has been very gratifying to the Committee, and it is planned to give a similar series annually hereafter. The fourth concert will be given on Tuesday, May 10, when an equally attractive programme will be presented.

Apart from its triteness and emptiness, the paragraph above is weak because of the structure of its sentences, with their mechanical symmetry and singsong. Contrast with them the sentences in the paragraphs quoted under Rule 9, or in any piece of good English prose, as the preface (Before the Curtain) to *Vanity Fair.*

If the writer finds that he has written a series of sentences of the type described, he should recast enough of them to remove the monotony, replacing them by simple sentences, by sentences of two clauses joined by a semicolon, by periodic sentences of two clauses, by sentences, lose or periodic, of three clauses whichever best represent the real relations of the thought.

15. Express co-ordinate ideas in similar form.

This principle, that of parallel construction, requires that expressions of similar content and function should be outwardly similar. The likeness of form enables the reader to recognize more readily the likeness of content and function. Familiar instances from the Bible are the Ten Commandments, the Beatitudes, and the petitions of the Lord's Prayer.

The unskillful writer often violates this principle, from a mistaken belief that he should constantly vary the form of his expressions. It is true that in repeating a statement in order to emphasize it he may have need to vary its form. For illustration, see the paragraph from Stevenson quoted under Rule 9. But apart from this, he should follow the principle of parallel construction.

Formerly, science was taught by the textbook method, while now the laboratory method is employed.

Formerly, science was taught by the textbook method; now it is taught by the laboratory method.

The left-hand version gives the impression that the writer is undecided or timid; he seems unable or afraid to choose one form of expression and hold to it. The right-hand version shows that the writer has at least made his choice and abided by it.

By this principle, an article or a preposition applying to all the members of a series must either be used only before the first term or else be repeated before each term.

The French, the Italians, Spanish, and Portuguese

The French, the Italians, the Spanish, and the Portuguese

In spring, summer, or in winter

In spring, summer, or winter (In spring, in summer, or in winter)

Correlative expressions (*both, and not, but; not only, but also; either, or first, second, third;* and the like) should be followed by the same grammatical construction, that is, virtually, by the same part of speech. (Such combinations as "both Henry and I," "not silk, but a cheap substitute," are obviously within the rule.) Many violations of this rule (as the first three below) arise from faulty arrangement; others (as the last) from the use of unlike constructions.

It was both a long ceremony and very tedious.

The ceremony was both long and tedious.

A time not for words, but action.

A time not for words, but for action.

Either you must grant his request or incur his ill will.

You must either grant his request or incur his ill will.

My objections are, first, the injustice of the measure; second, that it is unconstitutional.

My objections are, first, that the measure is unjust; second, that it is unconstitutional.

See also the third example under Rule 12 and the last under Rule 13.

It may be asked, what if a writer needs to express a very large number of similar ideas, say twenty? Must he write twenty consecutive sentences of the same pattern? On closer examination he will probably find that the difficulty is imaginary, that his twenty ideas can be classified in groups and that he need apply the principle only within each group. Otherwise, he had best avoid difficulty by putting his statements in the form of a table.

16. Keep related words together.

The position of the words in a sentence is the principal means of showing their relationship. The writer must therefore, so far as possible, bring together the words, and groups of words, that are related in thought, and keep apart those which are not so related.

The subject of a sentence and the principal verb should not, as a rule, be separated by a phrase or clause that can be transferred to the beginning.

Wordsworth, in the fifth book of The Excursion, gives a minute description of this church.

In the fifth book of The Excursion, Wordsworth gives a minute description of this church.

Cast iron, when treated in a Bessemer converter, is changed into steel.

By treatment in a Bessemer converter, cast iron is changed into steel.

The objection is that the interposed phrase or clause needlessly interrupts the natural order of the main clause. Usually, however, this objection does not hold when the order is interrupted only by a relative clause or by an expression in apposition. Nor does it hold in periodic sentences in which the interruption is a deliberately used means of creating suspense (see examples under Rule 18).

The relative pronoun should come, as a rule, immediately after its antecedent.

There was a look in his eye that boded mischief.

In his eye was a look that boded mischief.

He wrote three articles about his adventures in Spain, which were published in Harper's Magazine.

He published in Harper's Magazine three articles about his adventures in Spain.

This is a portrait of Benjamin Harrison, grandson of William Henry Harrison, who became President in 1889.

This is a portrait of Benjamin Harrison, grandson of William Henry Harrison. He became President in 1889.

If the antecedent consists of a group of words, the relative comes at the end of the group, unless this would cause ambiguity.

The Superintendent of the Chicago Division, who

A proposal to amend the Sherman Act, which has been variously judged.

A proposal, which has been variously judged, to amend the

Sherman Act.

A proposal to amend the much-debated Sherman Act.

The grandson of William Henry Harrison, who

William Henry Harrison's grandson, who

A noun in apposition may come between antecedent and relative, because in such a combination no real ambiguity can arise.

The Duke of York, his brother, who was regarded with hostility by the Whigs

Modifiers should come, if possible, next to the word they modify. If several expressions modify the same word, they should be so arranged that no wrong relation is suggested.

All the members were not present.

Not all the members were present.

He only found two mistakes.

He found only two mistakes.

Major R. E. Joyce will give a lecture on Tuesday evening in Bailey Hall, to which the public is invited, on "My Experiences in Mesopotamia" at eight P. M.

On Tuesday evening at eight P. M., Major R. E. Joyce will give in Bailey Hall a lecture on "My Experiences in Mesopotamia." The public is invited.

17. In summaries, keep to one tense.

In summarizing the action of a drama, the writer should always use the present tense. In summarizing a poem, story, or novel, he should preferably use the present, though he may use the past if he prefers. If the summary is in the present tense, antecedent action should be expressed by the perfect, if in the past, by the past perfect.

An unforeseen chance prevents Friar John from delivering Friar Lawrence's letter to Romeo. Meanwhile, owing to her father's arbitrary change of the day set for her wedding, Juliet has been compelled to drink the potion on Tuesday night, with the result that Balthasar informs Romeo of her supposed death before Friar Lawrence learns of the non-delivery of the letter.

But whichever tense be used in the summary, a past tense in indirect discourse or in indirect question remains unchanged.

The Friar confesses that it was he who married them.

Apart from the exceptions noted, whichever tense the writer chooses, he should use throughout. Shifting from one tense to the other gives the appearance of uncertainty and irresolution (compare Rule 15).

In presenting the statements or the thought of someone else, as in summarizing an essay or reporting a speech, the writer should avoid intercalating such expressions as "he said," "he stated," "the speaker added," "the speaker then went on to say," "the author also thinks," or the like. He should indicate clearly at the outset, once for all, that what follows is summary, and then waste no words in repeating the notification.

In notebooks, in newspapers, in handbooks of literature, summaries of one kind or another may be indispensable, and for children in primary schools it is a useful exercise to retell a story in their own words. But in the criticism or interpretation of literature the writer should be careful to avoid dropping into summary. He may find it necessary to devote one or two sentences to indicating the subject, or the opening situation, of the work he is discussing; he may cite numerous details to illustrate its qualities. But he should aim to write an orderly discussion supported by evidence, not a summary with occasional comment. Similarly, if the scope of his discussion includes a number of works, he will as a rule do better not to take them up singly in chronological order, but to aim from the beginning at establishing general conclusions.

18. Place the emphatic words of a sentence at the end.

The proper place in the sentence for the word, or group of words, which the writer desires to make most prominent is usually the end.

Humanity has hardly advanced in fortitude since that time, though it has advanced in many other ways.

Humanity, since that time, has advanced in many other ways, but it has hardly advanced in fortitude.

This steel is principally used for making razors, because of its hardness.

Because of its hardness, this steel is principally used in making razors.

The word or group of words entitled to this position of prominence is usually the logical predicate, that is, the *new* element in the sentence, as it is in the second example.

The effectiveness of the periodic sentence arises from the prominence which it gives to the main statement.

Four centuries ago, Christopher Columbus, one of the Italian mariners whom the decline of their own republics had put at the service of the world and of adventure, seeking for Spain a westward passage to the Indies as a set-off against the achievements of Portuguese discoverers, lighted on America.

With these hopes and in this belief, I would urge you, laying aside all hindrance, thrusting away all private aims, to devote yourself unswervingly and unflinchingly to the vigorous and successful prosecution of this war.

The other prominent position in the sentence is the beginning. Any element in the sentence, other than the subject, may become emphatic when placed first.

Deceit or treachery he could never forgive.

So vast and rude, fretted by the action of nearly three thousand years, the fragments of this architecture may often seem, at first sight, like works of nature.

A subject coming first in its sentence may be emphatic, but hardly by its position alone. In the sentence,

Great kings worshipped at his shrine,

the emphasis upon *kings* arises largely from its meaning and from the context. To receive special emphasis, the subject of a sentence must take the position of the predicate.

Through the middle of the valley flowed a winding stream.

The principle that the proper place for what is to be made most prominent is the end applies equally to the words of a sentence, to the sentences of a paragraph, and to the paragraphs of a composition.

IV. A FEW MATTERS OF FORM

Headings. Leave a blank line, or its equivalent in space, after the title or heading of a manuscript. On succeeding pages, if using ruled paper, begin on the first line.

Numerals. Do not spell out dates or other serial numbers. Write them in figures or in Roman notation, as may be appropriate.

August 9, 1918 (9 August 1918)

Rule 3

Chapter XII

352nd Infantry

Parentheses. A sentence containing an expression in parenthesis is punctuated, outside of the marks of parenthesis, exactly as if the expression in parenthesis were absent. The expression within is punctuated as if it stood by itself, except that the final stop is omitted unless it is a question mark or an exclamation point.

I went to his house yesterday (my third attempt to see him), but he had left town.

He declares (and why should we doubt his good faith?) that he is now certain of success.

(When a wholly detached expression or sentence is parenthesized, the final stop comes before the last mark of parenthesis.)

Quotations. Formal quotations, cited as documentary evidence, are introduced by a colon and enclosed in quotation marks.

The provision of the Constitution is: "No tax or duty shall be laid on articles exported from any state."

Quotations grammatically in apposition or the direct objects of verbs are preceded by a comma and enclosed in quotation marks.

I recall the maxim of La Rochefoucauld, "Gratitude is a lively sense of benefits to come."

Aristotle says, "Art is an imitation of nature."

Quotations of an entire line, or more, of verse, are begun on a fresh line and centered, but need not be enclosed in quotation marks.

Wordsworth's enthusiasm for the Revolution was at first unbounded:

Bliss was it in that dawn to be alive,
But to be young was very heaven!

Quotations introduced by *that* are regarded as in indirect discourse and not enclosed in quotation marks.

Keats declares that beauty is truth, truth beauty.

Proverbial expressions and familiar phrases of literary origin require no quotation marks.

These are the times that try men's souls.

He lives far from the madding crowd.

The same is true of colloquialisms and slang.

References. In scholarly work requiring exact references, abbreviate titles that occur frequently, giving the full forms in an alphabetical list at the end. As a general practice, give the references in parenthesis or in footnotes, not in the body of the sentence. Omit the words act, scene, line, book, volume, page, except when referring by only one of them. Punctuate as indicated below.

In the second scene of the third act

In III.ii (still better, simply insert III.ii in parenthesis at the proper place in the sentence)

After the killing of Polonius, Hamlet is placed under guard (IV.ii. 14).

2 Samuel i:17–27

Othello II.iii. 264–267, III.iii. 155–161.

Syllabication. If there is room at the end of a line for one or more syllables of a word, but not for the whole word, divide the word, unless this involves cutting off only a single letter, or cutting off only two letters of a long word. No hard and fast rule for all words can be laid down. The principles most frequently applicable are:

(a) Divide the word according to its formation:

know-ledge (not knowl-edge); Shake-speare (not Shakes-peare); de-scribe (not des-cribe); atmo-sphere (not atmos-phere);

(b) Divide "on the vowel:"

edi-ble (not ed-ible); propo-sition; ordi-nary; espe-cial; reli-gious; oppo-nents; regu-lar; classi-fi-ca-tion (three divisions allowable); deco-rative; presi-dent;

(c) Divide between double letters, unless they come at the end of the simple form of the word:

Apen-nines; Cincin-nati; refer-ring; but tell-ing.

(d) Do not divide before final *-ed* if the e is silent:

treat-ed (but not roam-ed or nam-ed).

The treatment of consonants in combination is best shown from examples:

for-tune; pic-ture; sin-gle; presump-tuous; illus-tration; sub-stan-tial (either division); indus-try; instruc-tion; sug-ges-tion; incen-diary.

The student will do well to examine the syllable-division in a number of pages of any carefully printed book.

Titles. For the titles of literary works, scholarly usage prefers italics with capitalized initials. The usage of editors and publishers varies, some using italics with capitalized initials, others using Roman with capitalized initials and with or without quotation marks. Use italics (indicated in manuscript by underscoring), except in writing for a periodical that follows a different practice. Omit initial A or The from titles when you place the possessive before them.

The Iliad; the Odyssey; As You Like It; To a Skylark; The Newcomes; A Tale of Two Cities; Dickens's *Tale of Two Cities.*

V. WORDS AND EXPRESSIONS COMMONLY MISUSED

(Some of the forms here listed, as *like I did*, are downright bad English; others, as the split infinitive, have their defenders, but are in such general disfavor that it is at least inadvisable to use them; still others, as *case, factor, feature, interesting, one of the most*, are good in their place, but are constantly obtruding themselves into places where they have no right to be. If the writer will make it his purpose from the beginning to express accurately his own individual thought and will refuse to be satisfied with a ready-made formula that saves him the trouble of doing so, this last set of expressions will cause him little trouble. But if he finds that in a moment of inadvertence he has used one of them, his proper course will probably be not to patch up the sentence by substituting one word or set of words for another, but to recast it completely, as illustrated in a number of examples below and in others under Rules 12 and 13.)

All right. Idiomatic in familiar speech as a detached phrase in the sense, "Agreed," or "Go ahead." In other uses better avoided. Always written as two words.

As good or better than. Expressions of this type should be corrected by rearranging the sentence.

My opinion is as good or better than his.

My opinion is as good as his, or better (if not better).

As to whether. *Whether* is sufficient; see under Rule 13.

Bid. Takes the infinitive without to. The past tense in the sense, "ordered," is *bade*.

But. Unnecessary after *doubt* and *help*.

I have no doubt but that

I have no doubt that

He could not help see but that

He could not help seeing that

The too frequent use of *but* as a conjunction leads to the fault discussed under Rule 14. A loose sentence formed with *but* can always be converted into a periodic sentence formed with *although*, as illustrated under Rule 4.

Particularly awkward is the following of one *but* by another, making a contrast to a contrast or a reservation to a reservation. This is easily corrected by re-arrangement.

America had vast resources, but she seemed almost wholly unprepared for war. But within a year she had created an army of four million men.

America seemed almost wholly unprepared for war, but she had vast resources. Within a year she had created an army of four million men.

Can. Means *am (is, are) able*. Not to be used as a substitute for may.

Case. The *Concise Oxford Dictionary* begins its definition of this word: "instance of a thing's occurring; usual state of affairs." In these two senses, the word is usually unnecessary.

In many cases, the rooms were poorly ventilated.

Many of the rooms were poorly ventilated.

It has rarely been the case that any mistake has been made.

Few mistakes have been made.

See Wood, *Suggestions to Authors*, pp. 68–71, and Quiller-Couch, *The Art of Writing*, pp. 103–106.

Certainly. Used indiscriminately by some writers, much as others use very, to intensify any and every statement. A mannerism of this kind, bad in speech, is even worse in writing.

Character. Often simply redundant, used from a mere habit of wordiness.

Acts of a hostile character | **Hostile acts**

Claim, vb. With object-noun, means *lay claim* to. May be used with a dependent clause if this sense is clearly involved: "He claimed that he was the sole surviving heir." (But even here, "claimed to be" would be better.) Not to be used as a substitute for *declare, maintain*, or *charge*.

Clever. This word has been greatly overused; it is best restricted to ingenuity displayed in small matters.

Compare. To *compare to* is to point out or imply resemblances, between objects regarded as essentially of different order; to *compare with* is mainly to point out differences, between objects regarded as essentially of the same order. Thus, life has been compared to a pilgrimage, to a drama, to a battle; Congress may be compared with the British Parliament. Paris has been compared to ancient Athens; it may be compared with modern London.

Consider. Not followed by as when it means "believe to be." "I consider him thoroughly competent." Compare, "The lecturer considered Cromwell first as soldier and second as administrator," where "considered" means "examined" or "discussed."

Data. A plural, like *phenomena* and *strata.*

These data were tabulated.

Dependable. A needless substitute for *reliable, trustworthy.*

Different than. Not permissible. Substitute *different from, other than*, or *unlike.*

Divided into. Not to be misused for *composed of.* The line is sometimes difficult to draw; doubtless plays are divided into acts, but poems are composed of stanzas.

Don't. Contraction of **do not.** The contraction of *does not* is *doesn't.*

Due to. Incorrectly used for *through, because of,* or *owing* to, in adverbial phrases: "He lost the first game, due to carelessness." In correct use related as predicate or as modifier to a particular noun: "This invention is due to Edison;" "losses due to preventable fires."

Folk. A collective noun, equivalent to *people*. Use the singular form only.

Effect. As noun, means *result;* as verb, means *to bring about, accomplish* (not to be confused with *affect,* which means "to influence").

As noun, often loosely used in perfunctory writing about fashions, music, painting, and other arts: "an Oriental effect;" "effects in pale green;" "very delicate effects;" "broad effects;" "subtle effects;" "a charming effect was produced by." The writer who has a definite meaning to express will not take refuge in such vagueness.

Etc. Equivalent to *and the rest, and so forth*, and hence not to be used if one of these would be insufficient, that is, if the reader would be left in doubt as to any important particulars. Least open to objection when it represents the last terms of a list already given in full, or immaterial words at the end of a quotation.

At the end of a list introduced by *such as, for example*, or any similar expression, *etc.* is incorrect.

Fact. Use this word only of matters of a kind capable of direct verification, not of matters of judgment. That a particular event happened on a given date, that lead melts at a certain temperature, are facts. But such conclusions as that Napoleon was the greatest of modern generals, or that the climate of California is delightful, however incontestable they maybe, are not properly facts.

On the formula *the fact that,* see under Rule 13.

Factor. A hackneyed word, the expressions of which it forms part can usually be replaced by something more direct and idiomatic.

His superior training was the great factor in his winning the match.

He won the match by being better trained.

Heavy artillery has become an increasingly important factor in deciding battles.

Heavy artillery has played a constantly larger part in deciding battles.

Feature. Another hackneyed word: like factor it usually adds nothing to the sentence in which it occurs.

A feature of the entertainment especially worthy of mention was the singing of Miss A.

(Better use the same number of words to tell what Miss A. sang, or if the programme has already been given, to tell how she sang.)

As a verb, in the advertising sense of *offer as a special attraction,* to be avoided.

Fix. Colloquial in America for *arrange, prepare, mend.* In writing restrict it to its literary senses, *fasten, make firm or immovable,* etc.

Get. The colloquial *have got* for have should not be used in writing. The preferable form of the participle is *got.*

He is a man who. A common type of redundant expression; see Rule 13.

He is a man who is very ambitious.

He is very ambitious.

Spain is a country which I have always wanted to visit.

I have always wanted to visit Spain.

Help. See under But.

However. In the meaning nevertheless, not to come first in its sentence or clause.

The roads were almost impassable. However, we at last succeeded in reaching camp.

The roads were almost impassable. At last, however, we succeeded in reaching camp.

When *however* comes first, it means *in whatever way* or *to whatever extent.*

However, you advise him, he will probably do as he thinks best.

However, discouraging the prospect, he never lost heart.

Interesting. Avoid this word as a perfunctory means of introduction. Instead of announcing that what you are about to tell is interesting, make it so.

An interesting story is told of

(Tell the story without preamble.)

In connection with the anticipated visit of Mr. B. to America, it is interesting to recall that he

Mr. B., who it is expected will soon visit America

Kind of. Not to be used as a substitute for *rather* (before adjectives and verbs), or except in familiar style, for *something like* (before nouns). Restrict it to its literal sense: "Amber is a kind of fossil resin;" "I dislike that kind of notoriety." The same holds true of *sort of.*

Less. Should not be misused for *fewer.*

He had less men than in the previous campaign

He had fewer men than in the previous campaign.

Less refers to quantity, fewer to number. "His troubles are less than mine" means "His troubles are not so great as mine." "His troubles are fewer than mine" means "His troubles are not so numerous as mine." It is, however, correct to say, "The signers of the petition were less than a hundred," where the round number a *hundred* is something like a collective noun, and *less* is thought of as meaning a less quantity or amount.

Like. Not to be misused for as. *Like* governs nouns and pronouns; before phrases and clauses the equivalent word is *as.*

We spent the evening like in the old days.

We spent the evening as in the old days.

He thought like I did.

He thought as I did (like me).

Line, along these lines. Line in the sense of course of procedure, conduct, thought, is allowable, but has been so much overworked, particularly in the phrase along these *lines,* that a writer who aims at freshness or originality had better discard it entirely.

Mr. B. also spoke along the same lines.

Mr. B. also spoke to the same effect.

He is studying along the line of French literature.

He is studying French literature.

Literal, literally. Often incorrectly used in support of exaggeration or violent metaphor.

A literal flood of abuse.	**A flood of abuse.**
Literally dead with fatigue	**Almost dead with fatigue (dead tired)**

Lose out. Meant to be more emphatic than lose, but actually less so, because of its commonness. The same holds true of *try out, win out, sign up, register up*. With a number of verbs, *out* and *up* form idiomatic combinations: *find out, run out, turn out, cheer up, dry up, make up*, and others, each distinguishable in meaning from the simple verb. *Lose out* is not.

Most. Not to be used for *almost*.

Most everybody	**Almost everybody**
Most all the time	**Almost all the time**

Nature. Often simply redundant, used like *character.*

Acts of a hostile nature	**Hostile acts**

Often vaguely used in such expressions as a "lover of nature;" "poems about nature." Unless more specific statements follow, the reader cannot tell whether the poems have to do with natural scenery, rural life, the sunset, the untracked wilderness, or the habits of squirrels.

Nearby. Adverbial phrase not yet fully accepted as good English, though the analogy of *close by* and *hard by* seems to justify it. *Near*, or *near at hand,* is as good, if not better.

Not to be used as an adjective; use *neighboring*.

Oftentimes, ofttimes. Archaic forms, no longer in good use. The modern word is *often*.

One hundred and one. Retain the *and* in this and similar expressions, in accordance with the unvarying usage of English prose from Old English times.

One of the most. Avoid beginning essays or paragraphs with this formula, as, "One of the most interesting developments of modern science is, etc.;" "Switzerland is one of the most interesting countries of Europe." There is nothing wrong in this; it is simply threadbare and forcible-feeble.

A common blunder is to use a singular verb in a relative clause following this or a similar expression, when the relative is the subject.

One of the ablest men that has attacked this problem.

One of the ablest men that have attacked this problem.

Participle for verbal noun.

Do you mind me asking a question?

Do you mind my asking a question?

There was little prospect of the Senate accepting even this compromise.

There was little prospect of the Senate's accepting even this compromise.

In the left-hand column, *asking* and *accepting* are present participles; in the right-hand column, they are verbal nouns (gerunds). The construction shown in the left-hand column is occasionally found and has its defenders. Yet it is easy to see that the second sentence has to do not with a prospect of the Senate, but with a prospect of accepting. In this example, at least, the construction is plainly illogical.

As the authors of *The King's English* point out, there are sentences apparently, but not really, of this type, in which the possessive is not called for.

I cannot imagine Lincoln refusing his assent to this measure.

In this sentence, what the writer cannot imagine is Lincoln himself, in the act of refusing his assent. Yet the meaning would be virtually the same, except for a slight loss of vividness, if he had written,

I cannot imagine Lincoln's refusing his assent to this measure.

By using the possessive, the writer will always be on the safe side.

In the examples above, the subject of the action is a single, unmodified term, immediately preceding the verbal noun, and the construction is as good as any that could be used. But in any sentence in which it is a mere clumsy substitute for something simpler, or in which the use of the possessive is awkward or impossible, should of course be recast.

In the event of a reconsideration of the whole matter's becoming necessary

If it should become necessary to reconsider the whole matter

There was great dissatisfaction with the decision of the arbitrators being favorable to the company.

There was great dissatisfaction that the arbitrators should have decided in favor of the company.

People. *The people* is a political term, not to be confused with *the public*. From the people comes political support or opposition; from the public comes artistic appreciation or commercial patronage.

Phase. Means a stage of transition or development: "the phases of the moon;" "the last phase." Not to be used for *aspect* or *topic*.

Another phase of the subject

Another point (another question)

Possess. Not to be used as a mere substitute for *have* or *own*.

He possessed great courage.

He had great courage (was very brave).

He was the fortunate possessor of **He owned**

Prove. The past participle is *proved.*

Respective, respectively. These words may usually be omitted with advantage.

Works of fiction are listed under the names of their respective authors.

Works of fiction are listed under the names of their authors.

The one mile and two-mile runs were won by Jones and Cummings respectively.

The one mile and two-mile runs were won by Jones and by Cummings.

In some kinds of formal writing, as geometrical proofs, it may be necessary to use *respectively,* but it should not appear in writing on ordinary subjects.

Shall, Will. The future tense requires *shall* for the first person, *will* for the second and third. The formula to express the speaker's belief regarding his future action or state is *I shall; I will* expresses his determination or his consent.

Should. See under **Would.**

So. Avoid, in writing, the use of so as an intensifier: "so good;" "so warm;" "so delightful."

On the use of so to introduce clauses, see Rule 4.

Sort of. See under **Kind of.**

Split Infinitive. There is precedent from the fourteenth century downward for interposing an adverb between *to* and the infinitive which it governs, but the construction is in disfavor and is avoided by nearly all careful writers.

To diligently inquire **To inquire diligently**

State. Not to be used as a mere substitute for *say, remark.* Restrict it to the sense of *express fully or clearly,* as, "He refused to state his objections."

Student Body. A needless and awkward expression meaning no more than the simple word *students.*

A member of the student body **A student**

Popular with the student body **Liked by the students**

The student body passed resolutions.

The students passed resolutions.

System. Frequently used without need.

Dayton has adopted the commission system of government.

Dayton has adopted government by commission.

The dormitory system **Dormitories**

Thanking You in Advance. This sounds as if the writer meant, "It will not be worth my while to write to you again." In making your request, write, "Will you please," or "I shall be obliged," and if anything, further seems necessary write a letter of acknowledgment later.

They. A common inaccuracy is the use of the plural pronoun when the antecedent is a distributive expression such as *each, each one, everybody, everyone, many a man,* which, though implying more than one person, requires the pronoun to be in the singular. Similar to this, but with even less justification, is the use of the plural pronoun with the antecedent *anybody, anyone, somebody, someone,* the intention being either to avoid the awkward "he or she," or to avoid committing oneself to either. Some bashful speakers even say, "A friend of mine told me that they, etc."

Use *he* with all the above words unless the antecedent is or must be feminine.

Very. Use this word sparingly. Where emphasis is necessary, use words strong in themselves.

Viewpoint. Write *point of view*, but do not misuse this, as many do, for *view* or *opinion*.

While. Avoid the indiscriminate use of this word for *and, but*, and *although*. Many writers use it frequently as a substitute for *and* or *but*, either from a mere desire to vary the connective, or from uncertainty which of the two connectives is the more appropriate. In this use it is best replaced by a semicolon.

The office and salesrooms are on the ground floor, while the rest of the building is devoted to manufacturing.

The office and salesrooms are on the ground floor; the rest of the building is devoted to manufacturing.

Its use as a virtual equivalent of *although* is allowable in sentences where this leads to no ambiguity or absurdity.

While I admire his energy, I wish it were employed in a better cause.

This is entirely correct, as shown by the paraphrase,

I admire his energy at the same time I wish it were employed in a better cause.

Compare:

While the temperature reaches 90 or 95 degrees in the daytime, the nights are often chilly.

Although the temperature reaches 90 or 95 degrees in the daytime, the nights are often chilly.

The paraphrase,

The temperature reaches 90 or 95 degrees in the daytime; at the same time the nights are often chilly,

shows why the use of *while* is incorrect.

In general, the writer will do well to use *while* only with strict literalness, in the sense of *during the time that.*

Whom. Often incorrectly used for *who* before *he said* or similar expressions, when it is really the subject of a following verb.

His brother, whom he said would send him the money

His brother, who he said would send him the money

The man whom he thought was his friend

The man who (that) he thought was his friend (whom he thought his friend)

Worthwhile. Overworked as a term of vague approval and (with not) of disapproval. Strictly applicable only to actions: "Is it worthwhile to telegraph?"

His books are not worthwhile.

His books are not worth reading (are not worth one's while to read; do not repay reading; are worthless).

The use of *worthwhile* before a noun ("a worthwhile story") is indefensible.

Would. A conditional statement in the first person requires *should*, not *would*.

I should not have succeeded without his help.

The equivalent of *shall* in indirect quotation after a verb in the past tense is *should*, not *would*.

He predicted that before long we should have a great surprise.

To express habitual or repeated action, the past tense, without *would*, is usually sufficient, and from its brevity, more emphatic.

Once a year he would visit the old mansion.

Once a year he visited the old mansion.

VI. SPELLING

The spelling of English words is not fixed and invariable, nor does it depend on any other authority than general agreement. At the present day there is practically unanimous agreement as to the spelling of most words. In the list below, for example, *rime* **for** *rhyme* is the only allowable variation; all the other forms are co-extensive with the English language. At any given moment, however, a relatively small number of words may be spelled in more than one way. Gradually, as a rule, one of these forms comes to be generally preferred, and the less customary form comes to look obsolete and is discarded. From time-to-time new forms, mostly simplifications, are introduced by innovators, and either win their place or die of neglect.

The practical objection to unaccepted and over-simplified spellings is the disfavor with which they are received by the reader. They distract his attention and exhaust his patience. He reads the form *though* automatically, without thought of its needless complexity; he reads the abbreviation *tho* and mentally supplies the missing letters, at the cost of a fraction of his attention. The writer has defeated his own purpose.

WORDS OFTEN MISSPELLED

- accidentally
- advice
- affect

- believe
- benefit
- challenge
- coarse
- course
- criticize
- deceive
- definite
- describe
- despise
- develop
- disappoint
- dissipate
- duel
- ecstasy
- effect
- embarrass
- existence
- fascinate
- fiery
- formerly
- humorous
- hypocrisy

- immediately
- impostor
- incident
- incidentally
- latter
- led
- lose
- marriage
- mischief
- murmur
- necessary
- occurred
- opportunity
- parallel
- Philip
- playwright
- preceding
- prejudice
- principal
- principle
- privilege
- pursue
- repetition

- rhyme
- rhythm
- ridiculous
- sacrilegious
- seize
- separate
- shepherd
- siege
- similar
- simile
- too
- tragedy
- tries
- undoubtedly
- until
- villain

Note that a single consonant (other than v) preceded by a stressed short vowel is doubled before *-ed* and *-ing*: *planned, letting, beginning.* (Coming is an exception.)

Write *to-day, to-night, to-morrow* (but not *together)* with a hyphen.

Write *any one, every one, some one, some time* (except in the sense of *formerly*) as two words.

LIST OF TITLES WITH ISBN NO.

ISBN	TITLE
9788194914129	1984
9789390575220	1984 & Animal Farm (2In1)
9789390575572	1984 & Animal Farm (2In1): The International Best-Selling Classics
9789390575848	35 Sonnets
9789390575329	A Clergyman's Daughter
9789390575923	A Study In Scarlet
9789390896097	A Tale Of Two Cities
9789390896837	Abide in Christ
9789390896202	Abraham Lincoln
9789390896912	Absolute Surrender
9789390896608	African American Classic Collection
9789390575305	Aldous Huxley: The Collected Works
9789390896141	An Autobiography of M. K. Gandhi
9789390575886	Animal Farm
9789390575619	Animal Farm & The Great Gatsby (2In1)
9789390575626	Animal Farm & We
9789390896158	Anna Karenina
9789390575534	Antic Hay
9789390896165	Antony & Cleopatra
9789390896172	As I Lay Dying
9789390896226	As You like it
9789390575671	At Your Command
9789390575350	Awakened Imagination
9789390575114	Be What You Wish
9789390896233	Believe In yourself
9789390896998	Best of Charles Darwin: The Origin of Species & Autobiography
9789390896684	Best Of Horror : Dracula And Frankenstein
9789390575503	Best Of Mark Twain (The Adventures of Tom Sawyer AND The Adventures of Huckleberry Finn)
9789390896769	Black History Collection
9789390575756	Brave New World, Animal Farm & 1984 (3in1)

9789390896240	Brother Karamzov
9789390575053	Bulleh Shah Poetry
9789390575725	Burmese Days
9789390896257	Bushido
9789390896066	Can't Hurt Me
9788194914112	Chanakya Neeti: With The Complete Sutras
9789390896042	Crime and Punishment
9789390575527	Crome Yellow
9789390575046	Down and Out in Paris and London
9789390896844	Dracula
9789390575442	Emersons Essays: The Complete First & Second Series (Self-Reliance & Other Essays)
9789390575749	Emma
9789390575817	Essential Tozer Collection - The Pursuit of God & The Purpose of Man
9789390896578	Fascism What It Is and How to Fight It
9789390575688	Feeling is the Secret
9789390575190	Five Lessons
9789390575954	Frankenstein
9789390575237	Franz Kafka: Collected Works
9789390575282	Franz Kafka: Short Stories
9789390575060	George Orwell Collected Works
9789390575077	George Orwell Essays
9789390575213	George Orwell Poems
9788194914150	Greatest Poetry Ever Written Vol 1
9788194914143	Greatest Poetry Ever Written Vol 1
9789390896301	Gulliver's Travel
9789390575961	Gunaho Ka Devta
9789390575893	H. P. Lovecraft Selected Stories Vol 1
9789390575978	H. P. Lovecraft Selected Stories Vol 2
9789390896059	Hamlet
9789390575022	His Last Bow: Some Reminiscences of Sherlock Holmes
9789390896134	History of Western Philosophy
9789390575121	Homage To Catalonia

9789390896219	How to develop self-confidence and Improve public Speaking
9789390896295	How to enjoy your life and your Job
9789390575633	How to own your own mind
9789390896318	How to read Human Nature
9789390896325	How to sell your way through the life
9789390896370	How to use the laws of mind
9789390896387	How to use the power of prayer
9789390896028	How to win friends & Influence People
9788194824176	How To Win Friends and Influence People
9789390896103	Humility The Beauty of Holiness
9789390896653	Imperialism the Highest Stage of Capitalism
9789390575084	In Our Time
9789390575169	In Our Time & Three Stories and Ten poems
9789390575145	James Allen: The Collected Works
9789390896189	Jesus Himself
9789390575480	Jo's Boys
9789390896394	Julius Caesar
9789390575404	Keep the Aspidistra Flying
9789390896400	Kidnapped
9789390896424	King Lear
9789390575824	Lady Susan
9789390896455	Law of Success
9789390896264	Lincoln The Unknown
9789390575565	Little Men
9789390575640	Little Women
9788194914174	Lost Horizon
9789390896462	Macbeth
9789390896929	Man Eaters of Kumaon
9789390896523	Man The Dwelling Place of God
9789390896349	Man The Dwelling Place of God
9789390575909	Mansfield Park
9788194914136	Manto Ki 25 Sarvshreshth Kahaniya
9789390896509	Marxism, Anarchism, Communism
9789390575664	Mathematical Principles of Natural Philosophy

9788194914198	Meditations
9789390575800	Mein Kampf
9789390575794	Memory How To Develop, Train, And Use It
9789390896486	Mind Power
9789390896585	Money
9789390575039	Mortal Coils
9789390575770	My Life and Work
9789390896035	Narrative of the Life of Frederick Douglass
9789390575152	Neville Goddard: The Collected Works
9789390575985	Northanger Abbey
9789390896530	Notes From Underground
9789390896547	Oliver Twist
9789390575459	On War
9789390575541	One, None and a Hundred Thousand
9789390896554	Othelo
9789390575435	Out Of This World
9789390575015	Persuasion
9789390575510	Prayer The Art Of Believing
9789390575091	Pride and Prejudice
9789390896561	Psychic Perception
9789390575381	Rabindranath Tagore - 5 Best Short Stories Vol 2
9789390575367	Rabindranath Tagore - Short Stories (Masters Collections Including The Childs Return)
9789390575374	Rabindranath Tagore 5 Best Short Stories Vol 1 (Including The Childs Return
9789390896622	Romeo & Juliet
9789390896127	Sanatana Dharma
9789390575596	Seedtime & Harvest
9789390896639	Selected Stories of Guy De Maupassant
9789390575206	Self-Reliance & Other Essays
9789390575176	Sense and Sensibility
9789390575299	Shyamchi Aai
9789390896738	Socialism Utopian and Scientific
9789390896646	Success Through a Positive Mental Attitude
9789390575428	The Adventures of Huckleberry Finn

9789390575183	The Adventures of Sherlock Holmes
9789390575343	The Adventures of Tom Sawyer
9789390896691	The Alchemy Of Happiness
9789390575862	The Art Of Public Speaking
9789390896288	The Autobiography Of Charles Darwin
9788194914181	The Best of Franz Kafka: The Metamorphosis & The Trial
9789390575008	The Call Of Cthulhu and Other Weird Tales
9789390575107	The Case-Book of Sherlock Holmes
9789390896110	The Castle Of Otranto
9789390896745	The Communist Manifesto
9789390575589	The Complete Fiction of H. P. Lovecraft
9789390575497	The Complete Works of Florence Scovel Shinn
9789390896820	The Conquest of Breard
9789390896813	The Diary of a Young Girl
9789390896332	The Diary of a Young Girl The Definitive Edition of the Worlds Most Famous Diary
9789390575701	The Great Gatsby, Animal Farm & 1984 (3In1)
9789390575312	The Greatest Works Of George Orwell (5 Books) Including 1984 & Non-Fiction
9789390575992	The Hound of Baskervilles
9789390896707	The Idiot
9789390896714	The Invisible Man
9789390575657	The Knowledge of the holy
9789390575558	The Law & the Promise
9789390896721	The Law Of Attraction
9789390896776	The Leader in you
9789390896363	The Life of Christ
9789390896196	The Man-Eating Leopard of Rudraprayag
9789390896783	The Master Key to Riches
9789390575268	The Memoirs Of Sherlock Holmes
9789390896479	The Midsummer Night's Dream
9789390575466	The Mill On The Floss
9789390896790	The Miracles of your mind
9789390896660	The Mutual Aid A Factor in Evolution
9789390896448	The Origin of Species

9789390896905	The Peter Kropotkin Anthology The Conquest of Bread & Mutual Aid A Factor of Evolution
9789390896806	The Picture of Dorian Gray
9789390896271	The Picture of Dorian Gray
9789390575275	The Power Of Awareness
9789390896356	The Power of Concentration
9788194824169	The Power of Positive Thinking
9789390575411	The Power of the Spoken Word
9788194914105	The Power Of Your Subconscious Mind
9789390896899	The Power of Your Subconscious Mind
9789390896417	The Principles of Communism
9789390575787	The Psychology Of Mans Possible Evolution
9789390896615	The Psychology of Salesmanship
9789390575732	The Pursuit of God
9789390575398	The Pursuit of Happiness
9789390896851	The Quick and Easy Way to effective Speaking
9789390575947	The Return Of Sherlock Holmes
9789390575138	The Road To Wigan Pier
9789390896981	The Root of the Righteous
9789390575855	The Science Of Being Well
9788194914167	The Science Of Getting Rich, The Science Of Being Great & The Science Of Being Well (3In1)
9789390896011	The Screwtape Letters
9789390896073	The Screwtape Letters
9789390575336	The Secret Door to Success
9789390575695	The Secret Of Imagining
9789390896868	The Secret Of Success
9789390896431	The Seven Last Words
9789390575930	The Sign of the Four
9789390896004	The Sonnets
9789390896516	The Souls of Black Folk
9789390896875	The Sound and The Fury
9789390575244	The State and Revolution
9789390896882	The Story of My Life
9789390896936	The Story Of Oriental Philosophy

9789390896752	The Strange Case of Dr. Jekyll and Mr. Hyde
9789390896943	The Tempest
9789390575916	The Valley Of Fear
9789390575879	The Wind in the willows
9789390896080	The Wind in the willows
9789390575763	Their eyes were watching gofd
9789390575831	Three Stories
9789390896950	Twelfth Night
9789390896592	Twelve Years a Slave
9789390896677	Up from Slavery
9789390896974	Value Price and Profit
9789390896967	Wake Up and Live
9789390896493	With Christ in the School of Prayer
9789390575602	Your Faith is Your Fortune
9789390575473	Your Infinite Power To Be Rich
9789390575251	Your Word is Your Wand
9789390575718	Youth
9789391316099	A Christmas Carol
9789391316105	A Doll's House
9789391316501	A Passage to India
9789391316709	A Portrait of the Artist as a Young Man
9789391316112	A Tale of Two Cities
9789391316747	A Tear and a Smile
9789391316167	Agnes Gray
9789391316174	Alice's Adventures in Wonderland
9789391316136	Anandamath
9789391316181	Anne Of Green Gables
9789391316754	Anthem
9789391316198	Around The World in 80 Days
9789391316013	As A Man Thinketh
9789391316242	Autobiography of a Yogi
9789391316266	Beyond Good and Evil
9789391316761	Bleak House
9789391316778	Chitra, a Play in One Act
9789391316310	David Copperfield

9789391316075	Demian
9789391316785	Dubliners
9789391316051	Favourite Tales from the Arabian Nights
9789391316235	Gitanjali
9789391316068	Gravity
9789391316150	Great Speeches of Abraham Lincoln
9789391316662	Guerilla Warfare
9789391316839	Kim
9789391316822	Mother
9789391316211	My Childhood
9789391316846	Nationalism
9789391316327	Oliver Twist
9789391316853	Pygmalion
9789391316334	Relativity: The Special and the General Theory
9789391316389	Scientific Healing Affirmation
9789391316341	Sons and Lovers
9789391316587	Tales from India
9789391316372	Tess of The D'Urbervilles
9789391316396	The Awakening and Selected Stories
9789391316402	The Bhagvad Gita
9789391316303	The Book of Enoch
9789391316228	The Canterville Ghost
9789391316907	The Dynamic Laws of Prosperity
9789391316006	The Great Gatsby
9789391316860	The Hungry Stones and Other Stories
9789391316433	The Idiot
9789391316440	The Importance of Being Earnest
9789391316297	The Light of Asia
9789391316914	The Madman His Parables and Poems
9789391316457	The Odyssey
9789391316921	The Picture of Dorian Gray
9789391316464	The Prince
9789391316938	The Prophet
9789391316945	The Republic
9789391316518	The Scarlet Letter

9789391316143	The Seven Laws of Teaching
9789391316525	The Story of My Experiments with Truth
9789391316532	The Tales of the Mother Goose
9789391316549	The Thirty Nine Steps
9789391316594	The Time Machine
9789391316600	The Turn of the Screw
9789391316983	The Upanishads
9789391316617	The Yellow Wallpaper
9789391316426	The Yoga Sutras of Patanjali
9789391316990	Ulysses
9789391316624	Utopia
9789391316679	Vanity Fair
9789391316020	What Is To Be Done
9789391316686	Within A Budding Grove
9789391316693	Women in Love